Low-Calorie Dishes

by Susan E. Mitchell

BARRON'S

Woodbury, New York · London · Toronto · Sydney

All inquiries should be addressed to:

Barron's Educational Series, Inc.
113 Crossways Park Drive
Woodbury, New York 11797

International Standard Book
No. 0-8120–5534-9
Library of Congress Catalog Card
No. 83-22465

**Library of Congress Cataloging in
Publication Data**
Mitchell, Susan E.
  Low-calorie dishes.

  (Easy cooking)
  Includes index.
  1. Low-calorie diet—
Recipes. I. Title. II. Series.
RM222.2.M544 1984   641.5'635   83-22465
ISBN 0-8120-5534-9

PRINTED IN HONG KONG
  4 5 6   490   9 8 7 6 5 4 3 2 1

Credits

Photography
Color photographs: Matthew Klein
Food stylist: Andrea Swenson
Stylist: Linda Cheverton
Sources for props: porcelain by Hutschenreuther,
  41 Madison Avenue,
  New York; stainless flatware from Georg
  Jensen, Inc., 683 Madison Avenue, New
  York; flowers by Howe, 171 West 23
  Street, New York City.

Author Susan Mitchell is a cookbook
  author, food/recipe consultant, and food
  stylist. She is a graduate of the Cordon
  Bleu School and a home economist.

Cover and book design Milton Glaser, Inc.

Series editor Carole Berglie

INTRODUCTION

Eating for health is in vogue. People today are focusing on fitness, and a good way to achieve and maintain that fitness is through a healthy diet. This new food awareness is affecting almost everyone, as we all count calories and cholesterol while we keep up with today's full-throttle life-style.

There are no secrets to losing weight and then keeping it off. You don't need to follow a starvation diet, nor do you have to try all sorts of confusing, esoteric fad diets. The truth is simple: if you want to weigh less, you must consume fewer calories than your body needs to maintain itself. If you follow such a regime, your body will eventually begin to use up the matter it has stored for a rainy day, and the pounds will begin to disappear. Once you reach your ideal weight, you will want to stay at that point; this means eating on a regular basis just about the exact number of calories your body needs to maintain its weight, given your level of activity. Of course, if you cut back on the number of calories you are consuming every day, you must be careful to choose foods that give you maximum return on your calorie investment—foods that are high in vitamins, minerals, and protein and that give you a feeling that you've eaten. Therein lies the rub! Just as you want to be a good shopper and spend your money wisely, so you will want to spend your daily calorie allotment wisely, and go to bed at night feeling that you've eaten well but not to excess.

Dieting is a very personal thing. What works for your neighbor may not work for you. If you like low-calorie foods to begin with, then weight gain has probably not been a problem for you anyway, but if you relish those creamy sauces and sweet desserts, then finding satisfactory diet foods can be a problem. Make dieting an adventure instead. Think of it as a chance to try new foods and to experiment with different ways of preparing old favorites. Use more fresh herbs and spices to heighten the natural flavors in foods. Perk up dishes with a dash of lemon juice instead of pouring on a fattening sauce. At the end of your diet, you may find that your food preferences have changed, so that maintaining your ideal weight becomes easier and more fun.

The recipes in this book are all low in calories. They range from soups to desserts, and vary in calorie count accordingly. All are based on the freshest of ingredients, presented imaginatively and simply—yet they are reduced in fat, sugar, and salt.

Butter and other fats are not only high in calories but also in cholesterol. As a general rule, I reduce all butter in recipes by at least half and cook with a little water or wine for liquid. I also often steam foods to release their vital juices while retaining more vitamins and flavors. Instead of thickening sauces with eggs, cream, or starches, I often use a purée of vegetables. Stocks and broths may be reduced until thickening by boiling down and evaporating the water to concentrate the flavors. When I do use a thickener, I use cornstarch or arrowroot to yield a lighter, clearer sauce at one-fourth the impact of flour (cornstarch and arrowroot have twice the thickening power and half calories of flour). Skim milk powder is also a quick and clever way to add protein and body to a white sauce without racking up a lot of additional calories.

Look to your markets for new products that can be used instead of the old standbys. Kefir cheese is now selling in many supermarkets as well as natural food stores; it is a creamy, low-calorie substance that will add flavor and body to foods. Neufchatel cheese, available on supermarket shelves right near the cream cheese, is a lower calorie spread that easily doubles for high-fat cream cheese. Substitute soured half and half for sour cream, and use canned evaporated skim milk instead of cream or regular evaporated milk. Buttermilk, low-fat cottage cheese, ricotta, and plain yogurt are relatively low in calories, and can be splendid bases for creamy dips and dressings in place of high-calorie oils and butterfats.

Sugar and salt have been implicated in many diet-related health problems, so these recipes tend to be low in those substances. Sugar is high in calories with little nutritional benefit, while salt increases one's blood pressure and helps to retain fluids in the body. Although salt is a necessary dietary element, most people consume far too much of it. Packaged foods especially are high in sugar and salt, and you'll have an easier time dieting if you avoid such prepared foods. Instead, rely on fresh ingredients themselves, or purchase foods that specifically state they are lower in salt or are sugarfree.

The cooking and preparation times for the recipes in this book are short, because practically no one has the time to spend long hours preparing meals. The techniques are also very simple, and with the step-by-step photos right alongside, you should have great success making these dishes. The full-page photos on the facing pages will show you how the finished dish looks, and will give you ideas on garnishing your meals so they are as appealing to the eye as they are to the palate.

Good food can be truly filling without fattening. Experiment with these low-calorie dishes, and experience the fun of eating fresh foods while you lose weight.

UNDERSTANDING THE RECIPE ANALYSES

For each recipe in this book, you'll note that we have provided data on the quantities of protein, fat, sodium, carbohydrates, and potassium, as well as the number of calories (kcal) per serving. If you are on a low-calorie diet or are watching your intake of sodium, for example, these figures should help you gauge your eating habits and help you balance your meals. Bear in mind, however, that the calculations are fundamentally estimates and are to be followed only in a very general way. The actual quantity of fat, for example, that may be contained in a given portion will vary with the quality of meat you buy or with how much care you take in skimming off cooking fat. If you are on a rigid diet, consult your physician. The analyses are based on the number of portions given as the yield for the recipe, but if the yield reads, "4 to 6 servings," we indicate which number of servings (4, for example) was used to determine the final amounts.

Desirable Weights

Height (without shoes)		Weight (without clothing)		
		Low	Average	High
	Men			
5 feet	3 inches	118	129	141
5	4	122	133	145
5	5	126	137	149
5	6	130	142	155
5	7	134	147	161
5	8	139	151	166
5	9	143	155	170
5	10	147	159	174
5	11	150	163	178
6	—	154	167	183
6	1	158	171	188
6	2	162	175	192
6	3	165	178	195
	Women			
5 feet	— inches	100	109	118
5	1	104	112	121
5	2	107	115	125
5	3	110	118	128
5	4	113	122	132
5	5	116	125	135
5	6	120	129	139
5	7	123	132	142
5	8	126	136	146
5	9	130	140	151
5	10	133	144	156
5	11	137	148	161
6	—	141	152	166

SOURCE: Consumer and Food Economics Institute, Agricultural Research Service, U.S. Department of Agriculture

DESIRABLE WEIGHTS

You can get an idea of what your desirable weight might be by using the table alongside. Locate your height in the left-hand column (without shoes). If you have a small frame, your weight should be no lower than the weight in the "low" column and no higher than that in the "average" column. If you have a large frame, use the "average" and "high" columns to determine your desirable weight range. If your frame is about average, your weight should probably be somewhere near the average for your height.

SALMON QUENELLES WITH CREAMY DILL SAUCE RECIPE

YIELD

4 servings

Per serving
calories 326, protein 38 g,
fat 15 g, sodium 368 mg,
carbohydrates 5 g,
potassium 828 mg

TIME

20 minutes preparation
20 minutes cooking

INGREDIENTS

1 pound fresh salmon fillets
½ pound scallops
3 egg whites
½ cup evaporated skim milk
Salt and freshly ground pepper
Court Bouillon (Recipe 9)
Fresh spinach, washed and trimmed
Lemon wedges
Dill sprigs (optional)

DILL SAUCE

3 ounces neufchatel or dietetic cream
   cheese
¼ cup plain yogurt
1 teaspoon lemon juice
1–2 tablespoons chopped fresh dill or
   1–2 teaspoons dill weed
2 tablespoons minced fresh parsley

Combine the first 3 ingredients in a food processor and add ⅓ cup of skim milk. Mix until thoroughly blended, adding the remaining milk if mixture is too dry. Chill. Prepare the dill sauce by combining all ingredients thoroughly in a blender or processor. Set aside. Bring court bouillon to a simmering point.

Steam the spinach ① until limp. Drain and reserve on a serving platter. Keep warm.

Using the salmon mixture, shape oval dumplings between 2 serving spoons dipped in cold water ②. Gently drop ovals into the simmering court bouillon and poach for 6 to 8 minutes. Turn and poach for another 6 minutes on the other side ③. As dumplings are finished cooking, place on the bed of steamed spinach and garnish with a little dill sauce, lemon wedges, and dill sprigs. Serve the remaining sauce on the side.

NOTE You may substitute cod, sole, red snapper, or any other firm whitefish fillets.

YIELD

4 servings

Per serving
calories 175, protein 12 g,
fat 3 g, sodium 374 mg,
carbohydrates 24 g,
potassium 530 mg

TIME

10 minutes preparation
10 minutes cooking

INGREDIENTS

1 tablespoon butter
1 carrot, peeled and diced
2–3 scallions, thinly sliced
1 tablespoon flour
1 can (13 ounces) evaporated skim
    milk
½ cup chicken broth
1 package (10 ounces) frozen petite
    peas, thawed
1–2 tablespoons dry sherry
Minced fresh parsley
Lemon slices

In a 2-quart saucepan, melt butter and sauté carrot and scallions ①. Add flour and cook, stirring, until foamy ②. Add the evaporated milk and the broth and bring to a boil, stirring occasionally. Add peas, reduce heat, and simmer until carrots are tender, about 6 to 8 minutes.

Whirl the soup in a blender, a portion at a time, until smooth (or force through a food mill or sieve) ③. Return purée to the pan, stir in the sherry to taste, and heat through. Serve hot or cold, garnished with minced parsley and lemon slices.

NOTE This is a light soup ideal as an hors d'oeuvre or first course.

3

YIELD

4 to 5 servings

Per serving (4)
calories 707, protein 37 g,
fat 40 g, sodium 1028 mg,
carbohydrates 50 g,
potassium 1163 mg

TIME

15 minutes preparation
25 minutes cooking
2 hours chilling

INGREDIENTS

½ pound shelled medium shrimp
1 teaspoon olive or safflower oil
2 cloves garlic, minced or crushed
1 small red onion, chopped
1 stalk celery, sliced
1 green pepper, seeded and cut into strips
1 cup brown or long-grain rice
1½ cups chicken broth
1 can (8 ounces) stewed tomatoes, with juice
Tabasco sauce to taste
1 whole chicken breast, skinned, boned, and slivered

1 chorizo or other spicy sausage, cut into 8 slices
1 avocado
Small red onion, sliced
Green leaf lettuce

DRESSING

⅓ cup safflower oil
⅓ cup lemon juice
½ teaspoon dried oregano or thyme leaves
½ teaspoon dry or Dijon-style mustard
¼ teaspoon garlic powder
¼ cup minced fresh parsley

Clean the shrimp, removing the veins ①.

In a large stockpot, heat oil and sauté garlic, chopped onion, celery, and green pepper just until softened, about 3 minutes ②. Add rice, broth, tomatoes, Tabasco, chicken, and sausage. Bring to a boil, reduce heat, cover, and simmer 15 minutes. Quickly add shrimp and cook 5 minutes longer, or until rice is tender and shrimp have turned bright pink. Remove from heat and allow to cool slightly.

Combine dressing ingredients in a covered container and shake until creamy. Place salad in serving bowl and add the dressing. Toss lightly. Refrigerate at least 2 hours. When ready to serve, peel, seed, and dice the avocado ③. Garnish with the avocado chunks, red onion slices, and lettuce leaves.

YIELD

4 servings

Per serving
calories 428, protein 58 g,
fat 10 g, sodium 567 mg,
carbohydrates 17 g,
potassium 1057 mg

TIME

10 minutes preparation
15 minutes cooking

INGREDIENTS

1 1/2 pounds chicken cutlets
Salt and freshly ground pepper
1 teaspoon each butter and oil
3 tablespoons finely chopped shallots
   or scallions
1/2 pound fresh mushrooms, quartered
   or sliced
2 tablespoons cognac or brandy
1 can (13 ounces) evaporated skim
   milk

1/2 cup shredded swiss cheese
1/2 cup crumbled low-fat farmers
   cheese
1/4 cup grated parmesan cheese
Minced scallions

Cut each chicken cutlet into 6 or 7 strips ①. Sprinkle with salt and pepper.

Heat the butter and oil in a heavy skillet and when it is foaming, add the chicken strips. Cook over high heat, stirring and shaking the skillet for 3 to 4 minutes ②. Remove the chicken with a slotted spoon and set aside.

Add the shallots or scallions, mushrooms, and cognac and cook, stirring, for 2 or 3 minutes. Add the evaporated milk and cook down over high heat for about 5 minutes. Stir in the cheeses ③. Add chicken and heat through. Sprinkle parmesan cheese over entire dish and run under the broiler until golden brown. Garnish with scallions and serve hot.

YIELD

4 servings

Per serving
calories 310, protein 23 g,
fat 21 g, sodium 464 mg,
carbohydrates 5 g,
potassium 263 mg

TIME

10 to 15 minutes
preparation
15 to 20 minutes cooking

INGREDIENTS

6 eggs, separated
2 tablespoons water
¼ teaspoon ground cumin
¼ teaspoon cayenne
1 cup ricotta
¾ cup grated monterey jack cheese
¼ cup grated romano cheese

FILLING

¼ cup diced canned green chilies, or
  2–3 fresh chilies, roasted, peeled,
  and minced
¼ cup Mexican hot sauce
2–3 tablespoons minced cilantro (fresh
  coriander)

Preheat oven to 425 degrees. Prepare the filling by mixing the chilies, hot sauce, and cilantro. Set aside.

With an electric mixer set on high, beat egg whites until they hold a stiff peak ①.

In a separate bowl, beat the egg yolks and add the water, spices, and cheeses. Mix well. Stir one-third of the whites into the yolk mixture ②. Then gently fold in half the remaining whites. Spoon the soufflé mixture into a greased 1-quart soufflé dish ③. Add filling and top with remaining soufflé mixture. Set dish into hot oven and bake until puffed and golden, about 15 to 20 minutes. Serve immediately.

YIELD

5 servings

Per serving
calories 106, protein 16 g,
fat 3 g, sodium 147 mg,
carbohydrates 1 g,
potassium 208 mg

TIME

15 minutes preparation
1 hour chilling

INGREDIENTS

1 pound peeled small shrimp, fresh or
   frozen
1 tablespoon neufchatel cheese or
   dietetic cream cheese
1 scallion
½–1 teaspoon lemon juice
⅛ teaspoon dill weed

MINCEUR MAYONNAISE

3 egg yolks
1 tablespoon Dijon-style mustard
2 teaspoons white wine vinegar or
   lemon juice
½ cup safflower oil
¼ cup kefir or neufchatel cheese
salt and freshly ground pepper

Thaw shrimp if frozen.

Prepare mayonnaise. Place yolks and mustard in blender or food processor ①. Whirl to blend, then slowly add vinegar. When blended, add oil a drop at a time, then increase flow to a slow, steady stream about ¹⁄₁₆ inch wide ②. Finally mix in kefir or neufchatel cheese and season to taste with salt and pepper. You should have about 1 cup. Measure 1 tablespoon for this recipe, then save remainder for other recipes.

Blend mayonnaise with neufchatel cheese. Mince the scallion ③, then combine with remaining ingredients for salad. Fold in shrimp and chill for 1 hour.

YIELD

4 servings

Per serving
calories 340, protein 21 g,
fat 9 g, sodium 433 mg,
carbohydrates 43 g,
potassium 1251 mg

TIME

10 minutes preparation
15 minutes cooking

INGREDIENTS

1 small red onion, thinly sliced
3 tablespoons butter
2 tablespoons flour
¼ cup nonfat dry milk
2 cans (13 ounces each) evaporated
   skim milk
1 cup skim milk
1 pound carrots, peeled and thinly
   sliced
¼–½ teaspoon dried thyme leaves

Sauté onion in butter over medium-high heat until soft ①. Stir in flour and dry milk ② and cook until bubbly. Gradually add evaporated and regular skim milks, stirring well to combine.

Add carrots to soup ③, and bring to boiling point. Reduce heat, and simmer until carrots are tender, about 10 minutes. Add thyme and season to taste. Place soup in blender and purée until smooth. Serve hot.

VARIATIONS For cream of asparagus soup, roughly chop 1 pound of fresh asparagus (save some tips for garnish). Add to soup base along with canned milk and simmer until tender, about 8 to 10 minutes. After puréeing, add dry sherry to taste and garnish with sieved hard-cooked egg yolk.

For cream of cauliflower soup, roughly chop 1 medium head of cauliflower. Add to soup base along with milk and simmer 10 minutes. After blending, stir in ½ cup shredded sharp cheddar cheese.

YIELD

4 servings

Per serving
calories 203, protein 22 g,
fat 10 g, sodium 273 mg,
carbohydrates 5 g,
potassium 582 mg

TIME

10 minutes preparation

INGREDIENTS

½ pound lean rare roast beef, sliced
1 medium cucumber, peeled in
   alternate strips
½ pound fresh spinach, rinsed and
   dried
½ cup kefir or neufchatel cheese
1–2 tablespoons freshly grated or
   prepared horseradish
1 tablespoon skim milk (optional)
1 teaspoon lemon juice
Salt and freshly ground pepper

Cut beef into thin julienne strips. Cut cucumber in half lengthwise ①. Scoop out seeds with spoon ②. Thinly slice ③ and add to roast beef.

Chop spinach and set aside.

Mix remaining ingredients and fold into roast beef mixture. On a serving platter, arrange chopped fresh spinach and add roast beef salad. Chill before serving.

YIELD

4 servings

Per serving
calories 349, protein 32 g,
fat 19 g, sodium 118 mg,
carbohydrates 3 g,
potassium 697 mg

TIME

10 minutes preparation
20 minutes cooking

INGREDIENTS

4 fish steaks or fillets, about 4 to 6
ounces each (sea bass, salmon,
snapper, or cod)
1 tablespoon cornstarch
Minced fresh parsley
chopped pimiento

COURT BOUILLON

⅔ cup each water and dry white wine
½ small onion, sliced
½ stalk celery, sliced
½ carrot, peeled and sliced
Bouquet garni (1 bay leaf, 1 sprig
parsley, 1 sprig or pinch thyme,
6 black peppercorns, tied together
in a cheesecloth bag)

Combine ingredients for court bouillon in a large saucepan. Bring to a boil, reduce heat, and simmer, covered, for 10 minutes.

Strain court bouillon through a fine sieve or cheesecloth into a large skillet ①. Place fish in hot court bouillon ②, then cover and simmer until fish becomes a creamy, opaque white and flakes easily when tested with a fork ③. The cooking time should be about 7 to 10 minutes, depending upon the thickness of the fish. Carefully remove fish to a heated serving platter.

To make the sauce, scoop up ¼ cup of bouillon and blend in the cornstarch until the mixture is smooth. Return bouillon to the pan and cook, stirring until bubbly and thickened. Pour sauce over fish and garnish with parsley and chopped pimiento.

YIELD

4 servings

Per serving
calories 461, protein 49 g,
fat 25 g, sodium 238 mg,
carbohydrates 7 g,
potassium 554 mg

TIME

15 minutes preparation
Overnight marinating
20 minutes cooking

INGREDIENTS

1 chicken, about 3½ pounds, cut up
1 cup plain yogurt
2–3 cloves garlic, minced or
    crushed
½ teaspoon each ground cumin and
    ground cinnamon
1 teaspoon each ground turmeric,
    ginger, and coriander
¼ cup minced red onion
¼ cup fresh lime juice
Salt and freshly ground pepper
4 lime slices

Prick skin of chicken with a fork ①. Combine remaining ingredients, except lime slices, in a large, shallow bowl and add the chicken. Coat chicken pieces with the mixture ②; cover and refrigerate overnight. Turn once during the marinating ③.

Preheat broiler or prepare coals for grilling. Place chicken on barbecue or broiling rack set 3 to 4 inches from the heat. Cook until crisp and cooked on each side, about 8 minutes per side. Serve with lime slices.

NOTE Chicken may be baked in a 375-degree oven. Place chicken on lightly greased baking dish, skin side up, and bake for about 45 minutes, or until tender.

YIELD

8 servings

Per serving
calories 428, protein 23 g,
fat 17 g, sodium 1695 mg,
carbohydrates 44 g,
potassium 274 mg

TIME

15 minutes preparation
4 minutes cooking
2 hours chilling

INGREDIENTS

4 quarts water
1 tablespoon each salt and oil
1 pound fresh pasta, preferably green
  or orange
½ pound cooked small shrimp
1 can (10 ounces) whole clams,
  drained
1 can (6 ounces) crab meat
1 red or green pepper, thinly sliced

1 small cucumber, peeled in alternate
  strips, then quartered and thinly
  sliced
¼ cup each capers, minced fresh
  parsley, and sliced ripe olives
½ cup kefir cheese
½ cup low-calorie Vinaigrette
  (Recipe 16)
Green leaf lettuce

Bring water, salt, and oil to a boil in a large kettle. Add pasta and cook about 4 minutes, or until *al dente*. Rinse, drain ①, and place in large bowl.

Add the remaining ingredients except the cheese and the dressing. Mix gently. Whisk the cheese and vinaigrette together to form a creamy sauce ②, then pour onto salad, toss gently ③, and chill for a couple of hours.

To serve, place salad in a large bowl and surround with green leaf lettuce.

YIELD

4 servings

Per serving
calories 522, protein 40 g,
fat 28 g, sodium 2218 mg,
carbohydrates 24 g,
potassium 1185 mg

TIME

15 minutes preparation
30 minutes marinating
15 minutes cooking

INGREDIENTS

4 chicken legs (thigh and drumstick), boned
½ cup oyster sauce
2–3 cloves garlic, crushed
1 tablespoon grated gingerroot
1 each green and red bell pepper
1 small zucchini
1 yellow crookneck squash
1 tablespoon sesame or safflower oil
1 red or yellow onion, sliced

8 flowerets each broccoli and cauliflower
¼ cup sherry or chicken or beef broth
1–2 teaspoons sambel oelek (Indonesian chile paste)
½ cup walnut halves
2 tablespoons tamari or regular soy sauce
Cooked brown or white rice

Marinate the chicken legs for 30 minutes in a mixture of oyster sauce, garlic, and ginger ①.

Slice peppers and squashes into julienne strips and set aside.

Over medium-high heat, heat the sesame oil in a wok or large pan until almost smoking. Add the chicken and onion slices and toss ②, cooking for 3 to 4 minutes. Add the remaining ingredients ③. Stir to mix well and cook until vegetables are tender-crisp. Serve over brown or white rice.

MARINATED SWORDFISH STEAKS

YIELD

4 servings

Per serving
calories 264, protein 30 g,
fat 10 g, sodium 1009 mg,
carbohydrates 5 g,
potassium 785 mg

TIME

5 minutes preparation
2 hours marinating
12 minutes cooking

INGREDIENTS

4 swordfish steaks, about 6 ounces
   each
2 teaspoons safflower oil
2 tablespoons tamari or regular soy
   sauce
1 tablespoon lemon juice
½ cup dry white wine
1 teaspoon chopped fresh tarragon or
   ¼ teaspoon dried
3 tablespoons minced scallions, white
   parts only

2 tablespoons Dijon-style mustard
2 tablespoons evaporated skim milk,
   kefir, or neufchatel cheese
Lemon wedges or slices

Place steaks in a shallow baking dish. Combine oil, soy sauce, lemon juice, wine, tarragon, and scallions, then pour over fish ①. Turn steaks to coat other side, cover, and refrigerate for 2 hours.

Blend together the mustard and milk or cheese ②. Preheat the broiler.

Broil steaks 3 to 4 inches from the heat for about 12 minutes or until fish browns lightly. During last few minutes, divide mustard mixture among the steaks ③, spreading a little on each. Serve with lemon wedges or slices.

YIELD

4 servings

Per serving
calories 475, protein 48 g,
fat 25 g, sodium 438 mg,
carbohydrates 6 g,
potassium 554 mg

TIME

10 minutes preparation
1½ hours cooking

INGREDIENTS

1 roasting chicken, about 3½ pounds
5 sprigs fresh dill or 1½ teaspoons dill
   weed
1 red onion, quartered
1 lemon, quartered
2 teaspoons butter
½ cup dry white wine
1 cup chicken broth
1 teaspoon cornstarch
Additional dill sprigs and lemon
   wedges to garnish

Preheat oven to 350 degrees.

Place chicken on roasting rack and put 4 sprigs (or 1 teaspoon dill weed) and quartered onion inside bird ①. Rub surface of chicken with lemon and spread with butter ②. Place 2 wedges of lemon inside, then place chicken in roasting pan and add wine and broth to pan. Roast for 1½ hours or until tender, basting with liquid every 15 to 20 minutes.

Transfer chicken from pan to a warmed platter and keep warm. Chop the remaining sprig of dill.

Strain the pan juices into a saucepan ③. Reserve 2 tablespoons of liquid and mix with the cornstarch until smooth. Pour cornstarch mixture into juices and bring to a boil. Whisk until smooth, add remaining dill and lemon, and then check for seasoning. Carve chicken and serve with sauce. Garnish with extra dill and lemon if desired.

SPINACH ROULADE WITH MUSHROOM FILLING

YIELD

4 to 6 servings

Per serving
calories 163, protein 12 g,
fat 10 g, sodium 258 mg,
carbohydrates 6 g,
potassium 563 mg

TIME

20 minutes preparation
10 to 12 minutes cooking

INGREDIENTS

1 package (10 ounces) frozen
  chopped spinach, cooked and well
  drained
2 egg yolks
Freshly ground pepper
Ground nutmeg
4 egg whites
1/3 cup freshly grated romano or
  parmesan cheese

FILLING

1/2 pound fresh mushrooms, sliced or
  chopped
1 teaspoon butter
1/2 cup kefir cheese or neufchatel
  cheese

Preheat oven to 375 degrees.

Mix cooked spinach with egg yolks. Season to taste with pepper and nutmeg.

Beat the egg whites until they form soft peaks. Stir one-third of the egg whites into the spinach mixture, then fold in remaining whites.

Line a baking sheet with buttered parchment paper or foil. Spread the spinach mixture on the paper or foil to a rectangle about 8 by 12 inches ①. Sprinkle with cheese and bake for 10 to 12 minutes.

Meanwhile, sauté mushrooms for filling in butter until just softened. Mix with cheese and set aside.

Turn out roulade onto a clean cloth or length of foil. Spread filling evenly over spinach, leaving 1/2 inch around the edge ② (so filling won't ooze out when rolled). Roll up ③. Slice and serve warm.

CRABMEAT AND ARTICHOKE SALAD

YIELD

4 servings

Per serving
calories 110, protein 8 g,
fat 6 g, sodium 658 mg,
carbohydrates 3 g,
potassium 185 mg

TIME

5 minutes preparation
2 hours chilling

INGREDIENTS

1 can (10 ounces) artichoke hearts
1 can (6 ounces) crab meat
1 can (2 ounces) sliced ripe olives
1 teaspoon grated lemon rind

LOW-CALORIE VINAIGRETTE

½ cup chicken broth
3 tablespoons vegetable oil
¼ cup plus 1 tablespoon red wine
    vinegar or lemon juice
1 teaspoon dry or Dijon-style mustard
Salt and freshly ground pepper

Combine ingredients for dressing in a small bowl and blend with a wire whisk ①. This will make 1 cup of vinaigrette. For this recipe you'll need ¼ cup; save the remainder for another use.

Drain the artichokes and crab meat ②. Combine artichokes, crab meat, olives, and lemon rind, then stir in ¼ cup vinaigrette ③. Chill for 2 or more hours.

NOTE If desired, add fresh minced parsley, chopped hard-cooked egg, or ½ teaspoon dried herb of your choice.

YIELD

4 servings

Per serving
calories 271, protein 8 g,
fat 2 g, sodium 483 mg,
carbohydrates 50 g,
potassium 419 mg

TIME

10 minutes preparation
25 minutes cooking

INGREDIENTS

2 red onions
2–3 zucchini
1 green pepper
1 tablespoon olive oil
3 cloves garlic, minced or crushed
1 can (16 ounces) whole tomatoes,
  drained
½ cup dry red wine
1–2 teaspoons chopped fresh basil
Salt
Freshly ground pepper
1 pound cooked pasta

Chop onions finely ①. Halve and then thinly slice the zucchini ②. Seed and core, then slice the green pepper ③.

Heat oil in large saucepan and sauté first onions, then zucchini and garlic until softened. Crush tomatoes and add, cooking briefly. Add remaining ingredients and simmer 15 minutes. Serve sauce over hot, drained pasta.

NOTE This sauce also works well as an accompaniment to lamb or pork chops, or as a filling for an omelet.

YIELD

4 servings

Per serving
calories 365, protein 55 g,
fat 11 g, sodium 276 mg,
carbohydrates 6 g,
potassium 555 mg

TIME

10 minutes preparation
20 minutes cooking

INGREDIENTS

8 chicken cutlets, about 2 pounds
¼ cup flour
¼ cup grated parmesan cheese
1 tablespoon each butter and
    safflower oil
8 thin slices prosciutto
8 thin slices provolone cheese

Pound cutlets to a thickness of ¼ inch ①. Stir together the flour and cheese, then coat chicken in flour-cheese mixture ②.

Heat butter and oil in a wide frying pan and sauté half the cutlets until golden (3 to 4 minutes per side) ③. Do not crowd pan or chicken will color unevenly. Keep cooked chicken warm while sautéeing remaining cutlets.

Preheat broiler. Top each cutlet with 1 slice of prosciutto and 1 slice of cheese. Broil until cheese is golden and bubbly. Serve hot.

FRUITED TOFU-SHRIMP SAUTÉ

YIELD

4 servings

Per serving
calories 198, protein 23 g,
fat 7 g, sodium 130 mg,
carbohydrates 11 g,
potassium 327 mg

TIME

5 minutes preparation
6 minutes cooking

INGREDIENTS

1 teaspoon each butter and safflower oil
2 cloves garlic, minced or crushed
⅔ pound shelled medium shrimp,
   cleaned and deveined
1 pound tofu, cut in 1-inch cubes
½ cup each red and green seedless
   grapes
¼ cup lemon juice
¼ cup minced fresh parsley
4 lemon wheels for garnish

In a large nonstick skillet, heat butter and oil over medium heat. Add garlic, shrimp, and tofu; sauté until shrimp just begin to turn pink, about 4 minutes ①.

Push food in skillet to edges of pan and warm grapes briefly in center ②. All at once, add lemon juice and parsley. Swirl pan to distribute juices and gently mix fruit with seafood.

Transfer mixture to a warmed serving platter or individual dishes and garnish with lemon wheels if desired ③.

YIELD

4 servings

Per serving
(without garnishes)
calories 293, protein 28 g,
fat 14 g, sodium 352 mg,
carbohydrates 13 g,
potassium 1018 mg

TIME

15 minutes preparation
30 minutes cooking

INGREDIENTS

1 pound lean boneless lamb
2 teaspoons butter
1 teaspoon safflower oil
2–3 cloves garlic, minced or crushed
1 onion, chopped
½ teaspoon each ground cardamom,
    coriander, and turmeric
¼ teaspoon ground cinnamon
¼ teaspoon minced gingerroot
1–3 teaspoons curry powder, depending on
    taste
1 cup plain yogurt
1 cup chicken broth
1 stalk celery, sliced
½ pound fresh mushrooms, sliced
½ pound asparagus or broccoli, cut in
    1-inch lengths
Cooked bulgur or rice
⅓ cup shredded raw carrots

GARNISHES

Unsalted raw cashews
Raisins
Plain yogurt
Kefir cheese
Sliced scallions
Lime wedges

Cut lamb into 1-inch cubes ①. Set aside.

Heat butter and oil in a large skillet, and sauté garlic and onion for 3 minutes, stirring often. Add lamb and brown cubes on all sides ②.

Add spices, yogurt, broth, celery, and mushrooms to skillet and simmer, covered, for 15 minutes. Add asparagus or broccoli on top of mixture in skillet and steam for an additional 10 minutes ③.

Place curry on a bed of bulgur or rice. Garnish with shredded carrots and serve with condiments, if desired.

YIELD

4 servings

Per serving
calories 353, protein 31 g,
fat 22 g, sodium 508 mg,
carbohydrates 3 g,
potassium 323 mg

TIME

10 minutes preparation
25 minutes cooking

INGREDIENTS

1 tablespoon safflower oil
2 cloves garlic, minced or crushed
8 chicken thighs
1 tablespoon lemon juice
1 tablespoon grated gingerroot
2 teaspoons arrowroot or cornstarch
1 tablespoon soy sauce
Salt and freshly ground pepper

Preheat oven to 450 degrees. In a heatproof and ovenproof casserole or skillet heat oil over medium-high heat. Sauté garlic briefly, then add chicken, skin side down, and sauté until golden brown, about 5 minutes ①.

Turn the chicken and distribute the lemon juice and ginger evenly over the chicken ②. Cover and bake in oven for 15 to 20 minutes.

Remove chicken from oven and place on a serving platter. Thicken the pan juices with a mixture of arrowroot and soy sauce ③. Season to taste and serve.

BEEF AND BROCCOLI IN YOGURT SAUCE

YIELD

4 servings

Per serving
calories 296, protein 31 g,
fat 12 g, sodium 463 mg,
carbohydrates 14 g,
potassium 983 mg

TIME

10 minutes preparation
Overnight marinating
8 minutes cooking

INGREDIENTS

1 pound flank steak, thinly sliced
1 tablespoon soy sauce
2 cloves garlic, minced
1 tablespoon grated gingerroot
¼ cup dry white wine or vermouth
1 tablespoon cornstarch
1 tablespoon safflower oil
1 bunch broccoli, flowerets and stems
    cut diagonally in bite-sized pieces
1 small red onion, sliced
1 cup plain yogurt
Minced scallions or fresh parsley

Marinate the steak overnight in a mixture of soy sauce, garlic, ginger, 2 tablespoons of the wine, and the cornstarch ①. Remove garlic and ginger, and discard. Reserve marinade.

Add half the oil to a very hot wok or frying pan, and stir-fry the broccoli and onion, stirring constantly until the broccoli turns bright green, about 2 minutes ②. Add the remaining wine, cover, and cook over high heat for 1 to 2 minutes. Turn onto a platter and arrange the flowerets pointing outward.

Heat the remaining oil and cook the beef slices, stirring constantly for 1 to 2 minutes, until brown. Add marinade mixture and stir in yogurt ③, then pour out onto center of broccoli. Garnish with minced scallions or parsley.

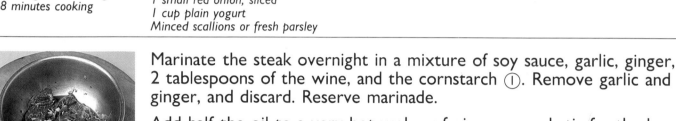

YIELD

4 servings

Per serving
calories 135, protein 6 g,
fat 4 g, sodium 510 mg,
carbohydrates 18 g,
potassium 523 mg

TIME

10 minutes preparation
40 minutes cooking

INGREDIENTS

1 small spaghetti squash
2 cups chicken or vegetable broth
1 pound baby carrots, peeled
1 tablespoon vermouth or dry white
   wine
1 teaspoon curry powder
1 teaspoon lemon juice
1 teaspoon minced fresh parsley
3–4 tablespoons kefir or neufchatel
   cheese

Cut the squash in half and place face down on a steamer (if halves won't fit into your steamer, cut in quarters). Steam squash until tender, about 30 minutes, then using a fork, pull strands from the squash to have "spaghetti" ①. Keep warm on a shallow serving bowl or platter.

Bring the broth to a boil. Add the carrots and cook, covered, for 8 minutes or until just tender-crisp. Drain and reserve stock.

Combine 2 or 3 tablespoons of the stock with the vermouth, curry, lemon juice, parsley, and cheese. Add carrots ② and toss gently ③. Serve atop the squash and then garnish with additional minced parsley if desired.

YIELD

4 servings

Per serving
calories 229, protein 22 g,
fat 5 g, sodium 186 mg,
carbohydrates 17 g,
potassium 597 mg

TIME

10 minutes preparation
30 minutes cooking

INGREDIENTS

4 loin lamb chops, each ¾ inch thick,
   trimmed
⅔ cup sliced red onions
⅔ cup beef broth
⅓ cup port or madeira wine
⅔ cup dried apricots or peaches
1 tablespoon grated gingerroot or
   ½ teaspoon ground ginger
2 teaspoons instant coffee powder
Salt and pepper
1 teaspoon cornstarch (optional)
Lemon or lime slices

In a large skillet, brown the meat with the onions ①. If meat is very lean, you may have to add a little oil.

Meanwhile, in a saucepan, heat the broth and wine and then add the dried fruit, ginger, and coffee ②, stirring to dissolve the instant coffee. Pour the liquid over the meat ③ and simmer, covered, for 15 to 20 minutes. Turn frequently to mix ingredients well.

Taste sauce and season to taste with salt and pepper. Thicken cooking liquid with cornstarch if desired, and garnish with lemon or lime slices.

YIELD

2 servings

Per serving (omelet only)
calories 195, protein 13 g,
fat 12 g, sodium 132 mg,
carbohydrates 2 g,
potassium 168 mg

TIME

8 minutes preparation
8 minutes cooking

INGREDIENTS

¼ cup skim milk
4 eggs, separated
1 tablespoon brandy
2 teaspoons butter
Savory Shrimp Salad (Recipe 6)

Beat together the milk, egg yolks, and brandy ①. Beat egg whites until they are stiff but not dry ②, then stir one-third of the whites into the yolk mixture. Gently fold in the remainder of the whites ③.

Preheat the broiler. Over medium-high heat, melt the butter in an ovenproof 9-inch skillet. Add the batter and cover. As the omelet cooks, slash it with a knife to the bottom of the crust to permit the heat to penetrate and cook the eggs. After 5 minutes, remove cover and transfer to the broiler to set the mixture. Broil until the omelet is a golden color, about 3 minutes.

Remove omelet from the skillet and pile on shrimp salad. Garnish with a sprig of dill or watercress.

YIELD

4 servings

Per serving
calories 87, protein 2 g,
fat 2 g, sodium 119 mg,
carbohydrates 9 g,
potassium 338 mg

TIME

20 minutes preparation
25 minutes cooking

INGREDIENTS

6–8 broccoli flowerets
2 carrots, peeled and diced
1/4 pound fresh green beans, trimmed
    and cut in small diagonal slices
2 teaspoons butter
2 tablespoons finely chopped shallots
1/2 red or green pepper, cut in julienne
    strips (optional)
2/3 cup dry white wine
Salt and freshly ground pepper
4 large iceburg lettuce leaves

Cook broccoli, carrots, and beans in simmering water for 8 to 10 minutes. Drain.

In a large skillet, melt butter and sauté shallots and peppers until softened. Add half the wine and cook over high heat for 1 minute. Mix in vegetables and season to taste with salt and pepper.

Preheat oven to 400 degrees. Bring 1 quart of water to a boil. Add the lettuce leaves and simmer for 3 to 4 minutes. Remove lettuce carefully, and spread out each leaf on paper toweling ①. Trim away a 1-inch-thick center rib from each leaf ②. Spoon the vegetable mixture evenly onto the center of each leaf. Bring sides of lettuce up over filling ③.

Lightly grease a shallow baking dish. Place the leaves, folded side down, in dish and pour in remaining wine. Cover dish with a lid or foil and bake for 10 minutes. Serve hot.

YIELD

4 servings

Per serving
calories 238, protein 8 g,
fat 8 g, sodium 183 mg,
carbohydrates 35 g,
potassium 1203 mg

TIME

10 minutes preparation
2 hours chilling

INGREDIENTS

1 papaya
2 medium cantaloupes
½ cup plain yogurt
½ cup kefir cheese
1 cup skim or evaporated skim milk
¼ teaspoon each ground cinnamon
 and nutmeg
Mint sprigs

Peel ① and seed ② the papaya. Cut the cantaloupes in half and remove seeds. Scoop out almost all of the flesh. Flute edges ③.

Place yogurt, cheese, skim milk, spices, and flesh of cantaloupes into a blender or food processor. Blend until smooth and creamy, then chill. Fill melon halves with soup and garnish with mint.

YIELD

4 servings

Per serving
calories 212, protein 3 g,
fat 2 g, sodium 37 mg,
carbohydrates 48 g,
potassium 854 mg

TIME

15 minutes preparation
2 hours chilling

INGREDIENTS

1 cup plain yogurt
¼ cup chopped crystallized ginger
2–3 tablespoons honey
1 teaspoon lemon juice
4 cups sliced mixed fresh fruits
    (strawberries, bananas, oranges,
    and so on)
4 sprigs mint

In a bowl, combine yogurt, ginger, honey, and lemon juice; mix thoroughly ①.

Pour mixture over fruits ② and cover. Refrigerate for at least 2 hours to marry flavors.

To serve, spoon fruits into small dessert dishes or parfait glasses. Garnish with a sprig of mint.

COLD CUCUMBER AND MINT SOUP

YIELD

4 servings

Per serving
calories 191, protein 8 g,
fat 15 g, sodium 254 mg,
carbohydrates 7 g,
potassium 283 mg

TIME

10 minutes preparation
2 hours chilling

INGREDIENTS

1 cup each plain yogurt and kefir
  cheese
2 cucumbers, peeled and coarsely
  chopped
1 teaspoon lemon juice
1 tablespoon chopped fresh mint
1 cup cold club soda
Salt
Freshly ground white pepper

Place yogurt and kefir in food processor. Briefly whirl to blend, then place cucumber and remaining ingredients in processor and process off and on until cucumber is finely diced. Season to taste with salt and pepper.

CEVICHE

YIELD

4 servings

Per serving
calories 123, protein 19 g,
fat 3 g, sodium 254 mg,
carbohydrates 4 g,
potassium 437 mg

TIME

10 minutes preparation
Overnight marinating

INGREDIENTS

1 pound combination of scallops, small
  shrimp, squid, and white fish fillets
2 scallions, minced
6–8 cherry tomatoes, halved
3 tablespoons lime juice
2 teaspoons oil
1 tablespoon chopped fresh cilantro
  (coriander) or parsley
1/4 teaspoon oregano leaves

Tabasco
Salt and pepper
Avocado slices

Combine seafood, scallions, cherry tomatoes, lime juice, oil, herbs, Tabasco, and salt and pepper to taste. Cover and refrigerate overnight. When ready to serve, place in serving bowl and garnish with avocado slices.

CITRUS FRUIT SALAD

YIELD

6 servings

Per serving
calories 98, protein 2 g,
fat 2 g, sodium 95 mg,
carbohydrates 18 g,
potassium 535 mg

TIME

10 minutes preparation

INGREDIENTS

1 bunch watercress, washed, dried,
 and stems twisted off
1 bunch escarole, washed and dried
2 each oranges and grapefruit, peeled
 and segmented
1/3 cup orange juice

1/4 cup lemon juice
1 tablespoon safflower oil
1/4 teaspoon dry mustard
Salt and freshly ground pepper

Break watercress and escarole into bite-sized pieces. Place in salad bowl, along with orange and grapefruit sections.

In a small bowl, mix together the orange juice, lemon juice, oil, mustard, and salt and pepper to taste. Pour over salad and toss gently.

COLIN'S COTTAGE-CHEESE MUFFINS

YIELD

8 to 12 muffins

Per serving
calories 240, protein 17 g,
fat 8 g, sodium 792 mg,
carbohydrates 24 g,
potassium 293 mg

TIME

10 minutes preparation
30 minutes baking

INGREDIENTS

3 eggs, lightly beaten
1 large onion, finely chopped
2 tablespoons soy sauce
1 tablespoon safflower oil
2–3 tablespoons nonfat dry milk
1 tablespoon wheat germ
2 cups low-fat cottage cheese
2 cups rolled oats
2 tablespoons minced fresh parsley

1 teaspoon ground sage
2 teaspoons Vegemite or tahini
 (optional)

Preheat oven to 375 degrees. Lightly oil a muffin tin.

Combine all ingredients in a bowl and stir well. Pour mixture into muffin cups and bake for 30 minutes. Serve warm.

INDEX